CaN·DoGS TALK?

Illustrated by Donna Gates

Written by Mary Shields

To Sarah

Jeff
2000

Volume 1 Alaskan Happy Dog Trilogy

pyrola publishing

Also by Mary Shields and available from Pyrola Publishing:
Sled Dog Trails, 1984
Small Wonders, 1987
This Year-Round-Alaska-Wall-Journal, 1986
Loving a Happy Dog, Volume 2 of the Alaskan Happy Dog Trilogy, 1992
Secret Messages—Training a Happy Dog, Volume 3 of the Alaskan Happy Dog Trilogy, 1993

Artwork by Donna Gates is available from:
Goose Lake Studio, P.O. Box 48, Denali Park, Alaska 99755

Acknowledgements:
My thanks to those who helped with this project: Rita Pitka, Ryan Binkley,
and Kathy Pearse—Ptarmigan Typing, Evelyn Trabant, Lincoln & Allen Book
Productions Manager: Richard Owsiany. And of course those wonderful dogs!
A special thanks to Dona Gates for her extra effort
on the illustrations and her calm patience.

Fifth Printing, 2000

Printed in the United States of America

ISBN 0-9618348-1-1 (Volume 1)
ISBN 0-9618348-2-x (3 Volume Set)
Library of Congress Number 92-82503

pyrola publishing

P.O. Box 80961 Fairbanks, Alaska 99708

Dedicated to Big Joe
and all his pups —
who shared their joy
and helped me to understand.

"Can too!"

"Can not!"

Rita and her friend Ryan were arguing.

"Let's go ask Mary," suggested Ryan. "She's raised sled dogs in Alaska for twenty years. She'll know."

"Can too!"

"Can not!"

"Good morning, kids," welcomed Mary. "What do you have to tell me today?"

"Good morning, Mary. Dogs can talk, can't they?" answered Rita, slipping out of her warm parka.

"Now that's a very good question. Come in and warm up next to the cookstove. These cookies will be ready to sample in just a few more minutes.

"I'll help you find your answer. Let's look at my big dog book." Mary took down the book and the kids gathered close.

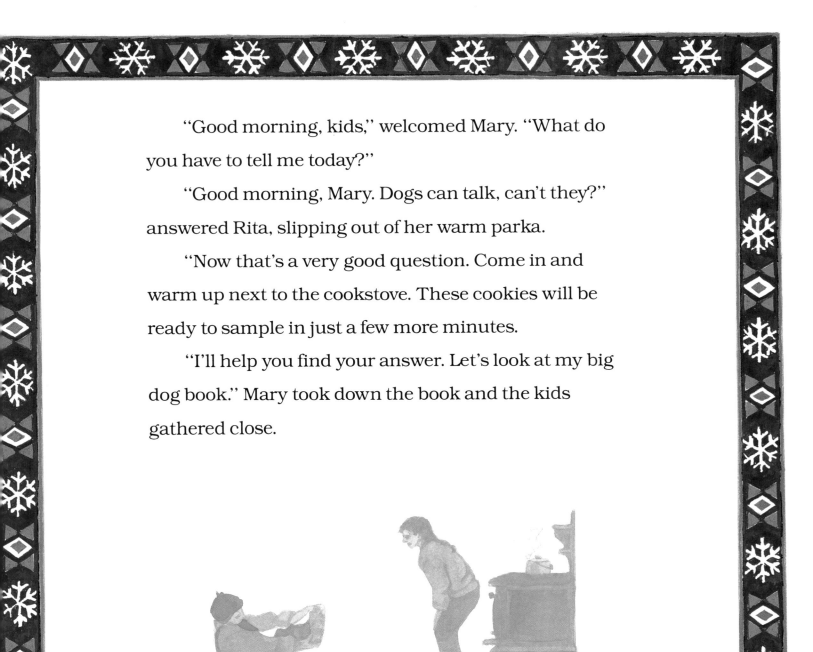

She read from the book:

Long, long ago, there were no dogs. But their ancestors, the wild wolves, lived together across the land. Wolves lived together in packs. They hunted together to find food. Wolves needed to talk to each other with their voices and their bodies, in order to live.

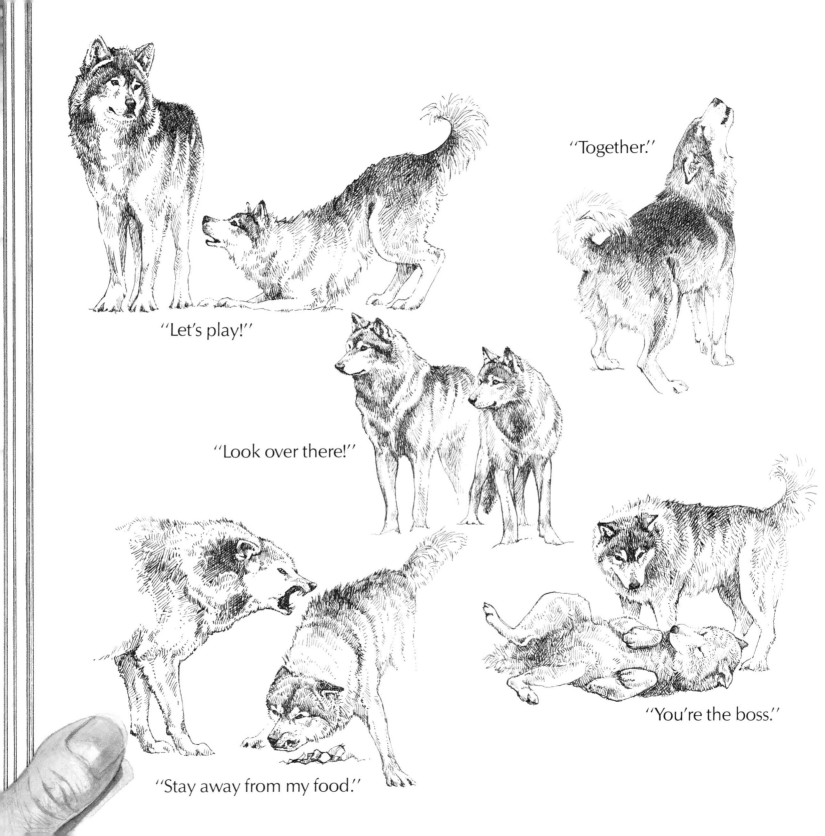

"Let's play!"

"Together."

"Look over there!"

"You're the boss."

"Stay away from my food."

Nobody knows for sure how the first dogs began. Perhaps a child found an injured wolf pup. The child cared for the pup and as the young wolf grew up, it joined the child's family.

Ever since that time, people have raised dogs for friends, and the dogs seem to really enjoy living with people.

"But do dogs talk?" asked Ryan.

"Let's look out the window and see if my dogs are talking to each other, just like wolves," said Mary. "Do they look like wolves?"

"Yes," answered Rita, "they look like wolves. Now can we go out and see if they can talk?"

Mary and the kids walked out to the dog yard.

The dogs leaped to their feet and danced around in circles, barking an eager greeting.

"The dogs are welcoming us," said Mary.

"They enjoy visitors as much as I do."

Mary introduced the kids to the first dog.

"This is Schnitzel, my number one lead dog."

"Good morning, Schnitzel! What do you have to tell us today?"

Schnitzel wagged and smiled and whined and yipped and wagged some more. He rubbed up against the kids, leaning into them.

"Schnitzel's very friendly," said Rita.

"He's telling us he likes us."

"Good morning, Jack! What do you have to tell us today?" asked Ryan.

Jack crouched over his bone, growled, and showed his teeth.

"I think Jack is telling us to stay away from his bone," said Ryan.

"He doesn't want to make friends right now."

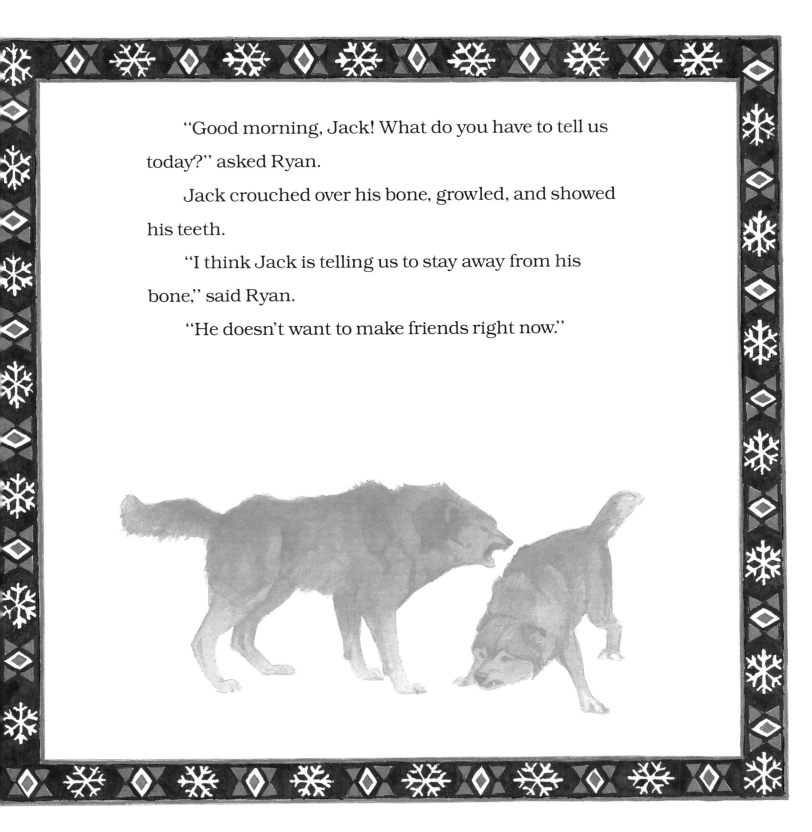

"Good morning, Flopsy! What do you have to tell us today?" asked Rita.

Flopsy lowered her head, tucked her ears back, and rolled over on her back. She showed her tummy for the kids to pet.

"Flopsy seems a little afraid of us," said Ryan.

"Yes," agreed Mary. "Flopsy is unsure of herself. She is a young dog. She's telling us she won't hurt us. Flopsy wants to be friends."

"Good morning, Joe! What do you have to tell us today?" asked the kids.

Joe jumped up on top of his dog house, barking at something he sensed out in the yard.

"Joe's telling us about something we can't see, out there by the dog sled. Let's check the puppies first and then we'll go look," said Mary.

"Good morning, Nellie! What do you have to tell us today?" asked Rita and Ryan.

Nellie paced back and forth in her puppy pen. She looked worried. She whimpered and kept peeking into her dog house.

"Quick, Rita!" yelled Mary. "Look and see if all five puppies are safe."

"One…two…three…four! I count only four puppies. That's what Nellie is telling us. One of her puppies is missing!" called Rita.

"We'll open the puppy pen and see if Nellie can tell us where her fifth puppy has gone," said Mary.

Nellie leaped through the gate and ran over toward the old sled. Mary and the kids chased after Nellie and there, under the sled, they found the fat little pup. The pup began to squeal. He was stuck between the runners. He couldn't go forward. He couldn't go backward.

"Good morning, little pup. What do you have to tell us this morning," teased Mary as the kids lifted the sled up and rescued the pup.

The puppy wiggled and wagged and cried and rolled over on his back as Nellie licked him all over.

"I think this puppy is telling us he is very happy to be out from under that sled," said Rita. "Let's name him HAPPY!"

"And Nellie is pawing me and wagging her tail," added Ryan. "She's saying 'thank you.' "

"Well, kids," concluded Mary. "I guess you've answered your own question: **dogs can talk!**"

"Can too!" agreed Rita.

"Can too!" admitted Ryan.

"Now," said Mary, "let's go back inside and rescue those cookies!"